The Guide to Owning

Eyelash and Temple Vipers

Ray Hunziker

CONTENTS

Title page: A nicely banded yellow and green Eyelash Viper, *Bothriechis schlegeli*. Photo: R. D. Bartlett

RE 152

© T.F.H. Publications, Inc.

Distributed in the UNITED STATES to the Pet Trade by T.F.H. Publications, Inc., 1 TFH Plaza, Neptune City, NJ 07753; on the Internet at www.tfh.com; in CANADA by Rolf C. Hagen Inc., 3225 Sartelon St., Montreal, Quebec H4R 1E8; Pet Trade by H & L Pet Supplies Inc., 27 Kingston Crescent, Kitchener, Ontario N2B 2T6; in ENGLAND by T.F.H. Publications, PO Box 74, Havant PO9 5TT; in AUSTRALIA AND THE SOUTH PACIFIC by T.F.H. (Australia), Pty. Ltd., Box 149, Brookvale 2100 N.S.W., Australia; in NEW ZEALAND by Brooklands Aquarium Ltd., 5 McGiven Drive, New Plymouth, RD1 New Zealand; in SOUTH AFRICA by Rolf C. Hagen S.A. (PTY.) LTD., P.O. Box 201199, Durban North 4016, South Africa; in JAPAN by T.F.H. Publications. Published by T.F.H. Publications, Inc.

MANUFACTURED IN THE
UNITED STATES OF AMERICA
BY T.F.H. PUBLICATIONS, INC.

THE SMALL PITVIPERS

INTRODUCTION

Welcome! Thanks for picking up this book—I'll try to make it worth your time.

If you didn't run screaming from the sight of the snake on the cover, it's obvious that you already have at least a passing interest in snakes. Although snakes are found in just about every habitat on earth with the exception of the polar regions, in this book we'll limit our study to a small handful of tropical, arboreal (tree-climbing) vipers. The two arboreal vipers that are arguably the most common in captivity because of their beauty and relative ease of maintenance are the Eyelash Viper, *Bothriechis* (formerly *Bothrops*) *schlegeli*, and the Temple Viper, *Tropidolaemus* (formerly *Trimeresurus*) *wagleri*. We'll concentrate largely on these two species, but we will also cover a good selection of their close relatives.

However, I'd like to make one thing very clear right up front: these snakes are not for amateur snake keepers. They are not even for the vast majority of expert snake keepers. Make no mistake: these snakes have the potential to kill you or, even worse, somebody else. Among other topics, we will definitely look at the legal and ethical ramifications of keeping "hot" (herper slang for venomous) snakes. This book series is called

The taxonomy of all the small vipers is in flux. Temple Vipers, *Tropidolaemus wagleri*, for instance, often are called *Trimeresurus wagleri*. Malaysian phase male. Photo: R. D. Bartlett

The Guide to Owning..., and we will cover captive husbandry in the interest of providing the necessary information on keeping these snakes alive and healthy to those who really need such information. However, I have no hesitation in saying that most of you reading this book should not even *think* about getting one of these snakes. I hope it will be enough just to know how it *could* be done. I hope that these caveats won't make you put the book down, because I think that these snakes are breathtakingly beautiful and that their natural history alone makes them worth looking at, even if you never keep one. Additionally, many zoos have fine reptile collections that include some of these species, so you can definitely enjoy seeing the snakes alive without keeping them yourself.

I have tried to use the most up-to-date taxonomy in this presentation, within reason. However, in many cases there is no universally agreed-upon taxonomy for some of the snakes in this book. The taxa are in a state of flux, constantly shuffled and reshuffled, with genera and species elevated, sunk, and otherwise modified. Many amateur herp hobbyists try to ignore scientific names completely, but I don't think that's possible at the expert level required of people who keep venomous snakes. However, don't think that just because a paper is published in a scientific journal it necessarily contains the Gospel truth about the animal(s) it concerns. Additionally, the opinion of any published "expert" is not necessarily any better than your own. They may be supported by a wealth of data, but they could still be wrong.

What I'd like you to come away with, more than anything else, is an appreciation for the beauty of these snakes. They are perfectly adapted to their natural environments and are not the demonic creatures of myth and legend. They're just animals, doing their best to survive in what can sometimes be a harsh world.

Let's start by considering just how these snakes are different from the rest.

WHAT ARE PITVIPERS?

The vipers, family Viperidae, are generally considered the most evolutionarily advanced of living snakes. They are divided into three subfamilies. One, an enigmatic southern Asian species called *Azemiops feae*, is of uncertain relationships and resides all by itself in the subfamily Azemiopinae. The balance of the vipers fall into two subfamilies: the Viperinae, or true vipers, which are exclusively Old World in distribution, and the Crotalinae, or pitvipers, which have both New World and Old World members. The snakes we will cover in this book are all pitvipers; although the viperines are also many and varied, we don't have the space to cover them here.

Pitvipers are quite variable, but in general they are massively built snakes with wide, triangular heads, short tails, and strongly keeled scales. The subjects of our book all hold to the general

Though colorful, few specimens of the primitive viper *Azemiops feae* reach the terrarium hobby. Photo: P. Freed

pitviper body plan except that they are more lithe and have longer, strongly prehensile tails. These are obvious adaptations for climbing.

The pitvipers are named for a unique feature: the loreal pit. Between the eye and the nostril is a deep pit in the loreal scale. This is an infrared heat sensor that is tuned to help the snake home in on warm-blooded prey such as small mammals. Other snakes have heat-sensing pits too (the boas and pythons, for example, have multiple pits associated with the rostral and labial [lip] scales), but the sensors of the pitvipers are considerably more complex. The pit contains a heat-sensitive diaphragm that is under the snake's conscious control. It can change the angle of the diaphragm to better zero in on prey. You can think of the pit/ diaphragm combination as a sort of radar dish that scans the environment and locks on to the strongest heat signatures. Now, consider that the snake has two of these organs, one on each side of the head, so that what its brain actually processes is a heat "image" in stereo, letting the snake accurately judge the distance to its prey and the prey's direction of movement. This is critical tactical information for making an accurate strike.

Infrared video has shown us some analogy of what the snake "sees" with its pits: the environment appears in cool blues and blacks, whereas a hot-blooded mouse or other mammal glows red, yellow, or even white. I suspect that the real thing is considerably more wondrous—the pitviper probably perceives a heat landscape as textured as the visual scenes we see with our eyes. It should come as no surprise that most pitvipers are strongly nocturnal; the heat of

Many small vipers have become arboreal, and all tend to look much the same. The bright green *Atheris chloroechis* of central Africa, for instance, looks like a strongly keeled *Trimeresurus* or *Bothriechis*. Notice that no pit organ is present between the nostril and the eye. Photos: K. H. Switak

day would probably make their heat-sensing pits unreliable at best. Also, of course, let's not forget that the snakes have perfectly good eyes too, with elliptical, catlike pupils that operate best in low light. Add to that a powerful sense of smell, aided by the flicking tongue that deposits scent samples from the air into the Jacobson's organ in the roof of the mouth. All in all, a pitviper has fantastically acute senses that put our relatively dull senses to shame. About the only things they don't have are external ear openings, so they probably don't hear airborne sounds; however, they do have ear bones that pick up vibrations transmitted through the lower jaws.

PITVIPERS AND VENOM

All vipers are venomous, and although the potency of the venom varies considerably from species to species, many have caused human fatalities, and ALL species, including the arboreal vipers we're covering in this book, must be considered potentially capable of doing so. (A word to the wise!) Venoms are produced by highly modified salivary glands, and the venoms themselves are really, then, just extremely weird saliva. Your own saliva has enzymes that help begin the digestive process; the venom of a pitviper is a complex soup of perhaps hundreds of enzymes and other proteins that do much more than digest. They attack the vital body systems of a prey animal on many levels to kill it quickly before it can escape irretrievably. It used to be said that snake venoms were basically of two types: hemotoxic (affecting the blood cells and vessels) and neurotoxic (affecting the peripheral nerves and even the central nervous system). We now know that this is a gross oversimplification. Just a few of the many compounds that viper venoms may contain are thrombolytic enzymes, which suppress clotting; thrombogenic enzymes, which *promote* clotting; proteases, which degrade proteins; bradykinin potentiators and histamine, which increase the inflammatory response (such as dilating blood vessels); hyaluronidases, which attack ligaments and tendons; acetylcholine, which disrupts nerve impulses; and even more exotic components such as deoxyribonucleases, which break down DNA. Ironically, many of these compounds are of considerable medical interest because when purified and administered in controlled doses they can treat a variety of human diseases. The blood-clotting components may be of use in treating hemophilia, for example, and the thrombolytic enzymes may have a role to play in treating stroke, phlebitis, or other occlusive vascular conditions.

The venom delivery apparatus of the pitvipers—indeed, of all vipers—is perhaps the most complex and advanced in the animal kingdom. The two maxillae—the bones at the front of the upper jaw—are hinged, and each is equipped with a fang. The

A stunning rusty phase *Atheris squamiger*, one of the more commonly seen tropical African arboreal vipers. Photo: R. D. Bartlett

fangs fold neatly into the roof of the mouth when not in use. The maxillae are hinged, and when the snake strikes it drops the lower jaw, rotates the maxillae upward to bring the fangs down, and stabs at its prey or attacker. The fangs are hollow and function much like hypodermic syringes. Once the fangs are embedded, the snake contracts small muscles to force venom from a poison gland under and behind the eye through the fangs.

The hollow fangs are unique among snakes and make venom delivery much more efficient. Other venomous snakes, such as the elapids (for example, cobras and coral snakes) have short, fixed fangs that conduct venom along an external canal, a deep groove that is not quite enclosed. The fangs of vipers are also replaced periodically, so the loss of one, even both, is not a life-threatening situation. A new fang grows into position behind the old one, eventually loosening the old one and forcing it out of the jaw. It is even possible, for a short time before the old ones drop out, that a snake will have *four* functional fangs. So, if you've ever heard that a venomous snake can be made safe by being "defanged," don't believe it. They don't stay that way permanently.

Many people think of venomous snakes as somehow evil, in large part because they "poison" their prey. Consider things from the snake's point of view, though. Predation is a dangerous business. Intended prey does not "go gently into that good night." Prey animals fight back. Fiercely. The lion may be killed by the

The loreal pit or pit organ is located between the eye and nostril in all the pitvipers, subfamily Crotalinae. It is very conspicuous in this terrestrial South American *Bothrops isabelae*. Photo: W. Wüster

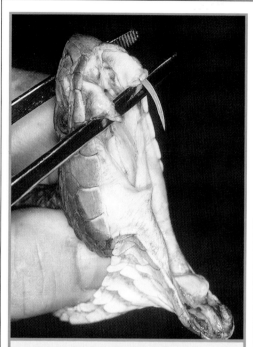

The fangs of pitvipers are long and curved and situated at the front of the upper jaw. All pitvipers are capable of a dangerous or deadly bite, depending on the size of the snake, its species (and venom composition), and the immunological reaction of the victim. Photo: P. Freed

Cape buffalo, and the snake may be killed by the rat. (Many a snake keeper has had the unpleasant surprise of having an angry rodent maim or kill a snake. That's why responsible keepers never feed live rodents unless the snake refuses all else.) Thus, venomous snakes, especially pitvipers, developed a better strategy. They strike fast and inject a quick-acting venom, then immediately back off. The prey may flee, but it won't get far before the venom stops it. Aided by its pit organs, the snake can track its prey to the spot where it drops. The snake's hunting strategy is elegant, really—venom allows the snake to obtain prey

with minimal risk to itself. Venom is not really meant to be used on humans; snakes would much rather use it on prey. Defensive striking is a last resort. However, don't presume on a snake's "good will." In essence, a captive snake is always "cornered" and could lash out defensively at any time.

Many people ask which snakes are the most venomous, or whether a particular species can kill a human being. There is no absolute answer to such a question, especially with vipers. Many factors come into play. First, envenomation is a question not only of the toxicity of the venom but of the amount injected. Even a mild venom may be lethal if enough of it is injected. Another factor is whether the snake is capable of delivering a full venom dose at a given instant. For example, if a snake has recently fed, its venom glands may be depleted and its bite may be "dry" or nearly so. It is even believed that pitvipers may have some degree of conscious control over the amount of venom injected, perhaps matching the amount injected to the size of prey or possibly varying the amount based on whether the strike is predatory or defensive. Variations in the human immune responses to a bite can also influence venom's toxicity. Some people will have a severe, even life-threatening allergic reaction (anaphylactic shock) to relatively mild venoms. I have seen some of the arboreal vipers described as having a bite "not much worse than a bee sting." This is probably an irresponsible over–simplification, but even if true of some vipers, let's not forget that bee stings kill hundreds worldwide every year.

YOUR SNAKE'S HEALTH

We don't have the space for an exhaustive list of the problems that can afflict captive arboreal pitvipers, but we can examine a few of the most common problems. Most of these will require that you seek the services of an experienced reptile veterinarian. A local herp society or nearby zoo may have the name of such a vet. However, long before you consider keeping any venomous snake, you should already be well acquainted with your vet through your years of experience with nonvenomous snakes. If you don't already know a reptile vet, you probably are not sufficiently experienced to keep hot snakes. Please, for heaven's sake, don't just show up at any random vet with a sick pitviper! They'll probably call the police. You can't assume that every veterinarian who hangs out a shingle is capable or willing to treat reptiles, and even fewer want to deal with hot herps.

One of the most common problems with captive arboreal vipers is dehydration. These snakes may be reluctant to drink from a bowl and must be misted

The venom glands of vipers begin producing venom before birth (or hatching in a few cases), so even hatchlings in the birth membranes can inflict a dangerous bite. All specimens of these snakes must be treated with great respect. Photo of *Bothrops alternatus*: P. Freed

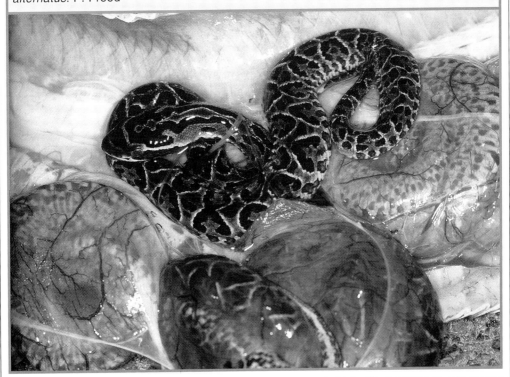

daily. This is especially important with wild-caught snakes. I don't recommend that you try to acclimate wild-caught snakes at all, but if you must try a rare species that is not yet captive-bred, be forewarned that they often arrive in an emaciated and very dehydrated state. They will be heavily parasitized as well, but this must take a back seat to rehydration first. Mist the snake as often as you can without making the cage a sopping mess, and make sure that you actually observe it drinking. In extremely severe cases intravenous rehydration by your vet may be necessary.

Failure to regulate humidity can cause a variety of skin problems. Snakes kept too moist may develop boils or blisters indicative of bacterial or fungal infections. Snakes kept too dry may have shedding difficulties such as patchy shedding or retained eyecaps. Patchy shedding can be alleviated by placing the affected snake and a damp towel

into a small, warm enclosure; the snake should be able to rid itself of the rest of its skin once it is humidified. Temple Vipers seem especially prone to dry skin, and some keepers routinely soak their snakes when molting is imminent.

Wild-caught snakes or those kept in unsanitary conditions in close proximity to wild-caught snakes may carry a heavy load of internal parasites such as roundworms and protozoans and external parasites such as ticks and mites. Newly acquired snakes, regardless of whether they are captive-bred or wild-caught, must be quarantined until it can be confirmed that they are eating and drinking properly. Mites can be dealt with using pyrethrin-based sprays, being cautious not to get any in the snake's mouth or nostrils. Protozoan parasites often respond to metronidazole; roundworms often require ivermectin. As with many drugs, kidney damage can result if the snake is not adequately hydrated during

The most commonly used substrates or litters for lining cages include pine shavings, processed paper pulp, and very fine aspen bedding.
Photo: G. & C. Merker

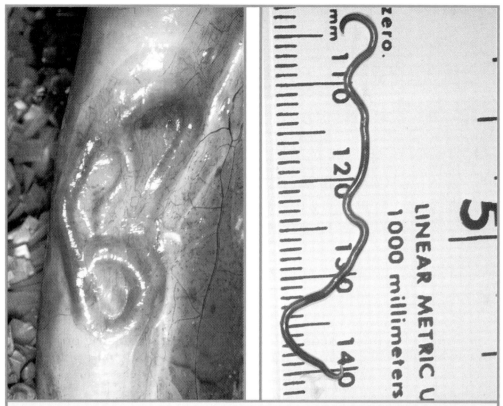

Pitvipers are notorious as carriers of many parasites. Autopsies often reveal tongueworms or pentastomes (top left) as well as a variety of nematode worms (top right), while many imports carry ticks of various sizes (bottom). Photos: P. Freed (worms), W. Wüster (ticks)

treatment, and proper dosing is a function of body weight. Need I say it? You'll need the vet again.

One of the most common and preventable problems in captive arboreal vipers is obesity. Remember that these snakes are ambush predators and that simply lying in wait perhaps 90% or more of their lives takes very little energy. Captive life is often an embarrassment of riches for these snakes, and although a fat snake may look like a happy snake, overweight snakes can develop a variety of health problems, particularly fatty liver damage and perhaps gastroenteritis. The timing of

feeding can be a little bit tricky, but adult Temple Vipers really need a good-sized mouse only every four to six weeks. Eyelash Vipers and the smaller *Trimeresurus* and *Bothriechis* can be fed a little more frequently, perhaps every month. Although it may sound a bit gross to contemplate, many professional keepers record when their snakes defecate and allow no more than two feedings per defecation. It makes sense, when you think about it—if you are feeding your snakes far more often than they are excreting, it is likely that they are putting on weight at an unhealthy rate. However, juveniles less than a year old should be fed more frequently, about every week (even twice a week if they are offered very small pinkie mice). Even if moderately overfed, most of the excess will go into growth.

Finally, perhaps the most insidious health threat is ophidian paramyxovirus, which primarily affects vipers and a select few other venomous snakes (although scattered cases in rat snakes and pythons have also been reported). This respiratory virus causes listlessness, gaping, loss of muscle tone, and "stargazing" behavior, where the neck curls over the back so the snake seems to be constantly looking at the sky. No cure is currently possible, although vaccines are being developed. Infected snakes must be euthanized and their cages sterilized to avoid transmission to other snakes in a collection.

Quarantine of newly acquired snakes is essential, and they should be quarantined as far away from established snakes as possible, because transmission is probably aerial.

ARBOREAL PITVIPERS

Now that we have a slightly greater respect for their potential, let's look at the real subjects of this book: arboreal vipers of tropical America and central to Southeast Asia. Tropical forests are well known as hotbeds of biological diversity, but why there are so many arboreal vipers in the tropics is something of an unanswered question. It's pretty certain that the ancestors of the tree-climbers were ground-dwelling snakes and not the other way around.

So why did they take to the trees? Were they trying to exploit an untapped food resource? Maybe. It's true that many species, especially as juveniles, consume treefrogs and small lizards such as anoles, and you won't catch them on the ground. Adult snakes will take birds, given the opportunity, and you won't get as many of them on the ground either. Were the snakes trying to escape ground-dwelling predators? That seems less likely, because a number of their kin stayed on the ground and thrived there.

Regardless of why they made the trip, arboreal vipers have been tremendously successful on several continents. Let's start with a look at the species that may be the most successful of them all, the Eyelash Viper.

THE EYELASH VIPER,
Bothriechis schlegeli

THE MOST COMMON HOBBY VIPER

A conservative estimate of the number of species of venomous snakes now regularly bred in captivity for the reptile trade would probably be in the dozens, perhaps even 100. Perhaps 100 more are intermittently available from captive-bred or wild-caught sources. Without a doubt, the species that is the mainstay of the hot herp trade is the Eyelash Viper, *Bothriechis schlegeli.* It is relatively small, very pretty, moderately easy to keep and breed, and is considered fairly mild-tempered as venomous snakes go. Keep in mind, though, that this placid demeanor can change at a moment's notice. Never let your guard down!

Eyelash Vipers are found from southern Mexico to northwestern South America (Chiapas, Mexico, and Belize south through Costa Rica to Panama, and then

Though small and generally placid, Eyelash Vipers can react unpredictably. Keep this in mind at all times when the terrarium is opened. Photo: R. D. Bartlett

Wet tropical forests of Mexico and Central America into northwestern South America are the main habitat of the Eyelash Viper, but it also can be found on coffee plantations that have replaced natural forests. Photo: Z. Takacs

through Colombia to Ecuador and Venezuela). They are often the most abundant venomous snakes in a given region, although this may not always be appreciated because most color phases are cryptically patterned and inactive by day. They inhabit moist to wet tropical forests from sea level to over 5000 feet (over 1500 m) but prefer the lowlands. Although they are arboreal, they do not often ascend to the tops of the largest trees, but prefer small trees and low bushes. Coffee trees are small, so it should come as no surprise that Eyelash Vipers are common there and are much hated by coffee growers and harvesters. The snakes also inhabit banana trees and palms, thus they and their relatives are often called palm vipers (which leads to some confusion with *Trimeresurus* and others, as we will see). We will use a more recent convention, "palm-pitvipers." It's a slightly odd construction, but it is memorable and distinctive.

These Neotropical vipers were once placed in the genus *Bothrops* along with the infamous Fer-de-lance (*Bothrops atrox* and similar species) and many others. About two decade ago, however, *Bothrops* was split into the genera or subgenera *Atropoides, Bothriechis, Bothriopsis, Bothrops, Cerrophidion, Ophryacus,* and *Porthidium.* The validity of most of these groups is still questioned by many herpetologists, and the latest findings through molecular biological studies have not always agreed with the morphological differences on which these groups were based. Some species could be equally well put in two of the groups, so sometimes you will see a species listed under two names. The conservative approach is to call all the species *Bothrops* still and wait for more evidence to back up the generic splitting, but much of the hobbyist literature and a good portion of the technical literature use *Bothriechis* for the arboreal species of *Bothrops*, and that is the course I will follow here, even if only tentatively.

The Eyelash Viper gets its common name from the row of raised superciliary scales placed between the row of seven to ten supraocular scales and the eye. These are small scales that form flattened spines and project up and slightly outward; there are usually two or three on each side, but they may be quite small in specimens from South America. To my eye they look more like horns, but if you have a little bit of imagination you can perhaps see them as "eyelashes." These are not just decorative—rather,

The prominent projecting superciliary scales (over each eye) or "eyelashes" gave rise to the common name of this species. Notice also the deep sensory pit in this yellow specimen from northeastern Costa Rica. Photo: Z. Takacs

Though hobbyists selectively breed Eyelash Vipers for the bright golden or oropel phase, the natural green phase (inset) also is appreciated by many keepers. Both have similar care requirements. Photos: Marian Bacon; J. C. Murphy (inset)

Red also sometimes is prominent in the coloration of the Eyelash Viper. This golden phase individual shows distinctly red dorsal blotches. Photo: K. H. Switak

they may serve to shield the snake's eyes from injury by prey animals or to shadow the eyes from bright overhead light.

As might be expected of an arboreal snake, the Eyelash Viper is far more slender than terrestrial pitvipers, but it shares with them a broad, triangular head and slender neck. Large wild females can grow to 40 inches (1 meter), but because they drape themselves in graceful coils over a branch when at rest, they often do not appear as big are they really are. Captive-raised specimens are frequently smaller, reaching about 30 inches (76 cm) in females and 24 inches (61 cm) in males.

The Eyelash Viper is one of the most variable of venomous snakes in color and pattern, although no single pattern is consistently tied to a particular geographic location; thus no subspecies are currently recognized. (One former subspecies, *superciliaris*, was recently elevated to a full species; more on that in a bit.) The color phase most popular with herpetoculturists is the golden or *oropel* phase. The most prized oropels are bright yellow to orange over the entire body, with few to none of the peppery black spots that are frequently seen in other color phases of the species. Oropels often have russet diamonds dorsally and laterally, as well as some facial striping. I personally don't like patternless snakes, so I prefer these patterned specimens, but many prefer the cleaner look of a patternless snake. Oropels normally breed true; that is, their babies are also golden. In nature this color phase is recorded only from a strip from Honduras to western Panama; there appear to be no South American or Mexican records.

Much more common than the oropel in wild populations but rarer in collections is the extremely variable "green" phase that comes in shades of olive with maroon diamonds dorsally. Also seen are pink, tan, or gray specimens and specimens with combinations of any of the aforementioned colors. At many herp shows I have attended, however, light-colored specimens were often lumped together as "gold" and dark-colored specimens lumped together as "green." There are some interesting phases available, however. Specimens with a lot of green, red, and white are often sold as "Christmas" phase. I'm especially fond of the "tiger" phase, which is evenly banded with bright yellow and bright green; I like them even better than oropels.

From the standpoint of breeding, gold usually begets gold, but mating gold and green specimens often results in a mix of colors, including some golds, and mating two greens (i.e., any two dark-colored specimens) will produce unpredictable progeny. Some may be very attractive,

Not as commonly seen in the terrarium as golden or green phases is the solid rusty red phase. Any of these colors can appear in a single litter from a mother of almost any color. Photo: K. H. Switak

These young Eyelash Vipers are all from the same clutch. The gray specimen probably will change color as it grows, though final adult coloration appears to be unpredictable. The golden young probably will remain golden. Photo: P. Freed

others not. Do not be surprised if the offspring are all gray at first. With the exception of oropels, which are born gold and remain some shade of gold their entire lives, other young Eyelash Vipers may change greatly in color and pattern as they grow. Give them time, as some of the dull babies may be diamonds in the rough. It is interesting to note that the eye color usually matches the body color: oropels have yellow eyes, mottled specimens have mottled eyes, and gray specimens have gray eyes, etc.

Eyelash Vipers consume a variety of small prey, but treefrogs and small lizards are high on their list. We will keep this in mind later when we talk about feeding captives. It might seem a waste of perfectly good pit organs to go for cold-blooded prey, but Eyelash Vipers are not overly specialized feeders, and adults will not hesitate to take small birds and mammals as well.

CARE IN CAPTIVITY

The captive care of Eyelash Vipers is pretty uncomplicated. The snakes like a tall, roomy terrarium that gives them plenty of room to climb. An enclosure of about 24L X 24W X 36H inches

(61 X 61 X 91 cm) is a good size for a pair or trio of Eyelash Vipers. Top ventilation is essential, and some side ventilation is desirable. Don't go overboard on the latter, though, as it makes it harder to maintain the high humidity levels these snakes prefer, and Eyelash Vipers must be protected from chilly drafts. Consider also the material from which the cage is constructed; inexpensive composites such as melamine are often used in building herp cages, but the high humidity necessary in what will essentially be a rainforest terrarium will warp melamine. Glass, fiberglass, and heavier-gauge plastics are unaffected by humidity.

Horizontally placed branches and boughs of various diameters should be positioned both low and high to permit the snakes to choose their own comfort level. Some keepers use wooden or plastic dowels, but other keepers feel that the snakes object to the smooth feel of these materials and prefer the better traction offered by natural, bark-covered branches. Regardless of what is used, an important consideration is that the perches should be easy to remove for cleaning.

The floor of the cage should be covered with a substrate that helps to retain moisture but does not pack down so tightly that it encourages bacterial and fungal growth. Potting soil and gravel are not recommended. Bark mulches are good choices. Orchid bark mulch, available in most pet stores under a variety of trade names, is about the texture of coarse gravel (pieces about one-fifth inch, 5 mm, in diameter) but much lighter in weight. I have used cypress bark mulch with a wide variety of humidity-loving herps with good results. Stay away from cedar and pine, which have aromatic tars and oils that may be irritating. As with all other cage contents, make sure that the substrate is easily removed and replaced. Some cages employ a drop-down panel at the front that lets the keeper remove the contents easily with a flat-edged rake at the end of a sufficiently long handle.

Eyelash Vipers may be skittish and irritable if kept in a cage with inadequate cover. If alarmed, they will display a stereotypical behavior called gaping, opening the jaws wide and displaying the white mouth lining. This is like the rattlesnake's rattle—a warning that the snake is preparing to strike if you don't back off. Most keepers put pots of hardy vining plants such as pothos or philodendron in their Eyelash Viper cages to give the snakes a greater sense of security. Silk or plastic plants will also work well if you don't have a green thumb. Regardless of which you choose, it is important that they are easy to remove from the cage. A good overall rule of thumb is that everything in the cage should be removable.

Ideally, the cage should open from the front, not the top, as this makes servicing the cage easier and safer for you. A partitioned door that swings or slides from

Most Eyelash Vipers in the hobby come from Costa Rican strains, but the species is widely distributed over Central America. This bright yellow specimen came from Panama. Photo: R. D. Babb

both sides is best, as it can let you choose to access a portion of the cage that the snakes don't happen to be in at the moment. Keepers have come up with a variety of devices for shielding themselves from their snakes to do routine maintenance. One that is simple but effective is a clear plastic "flyswatter" that is held in front of the snake to keep it confined. Essentially this is a rectangle of heavy plastic screwed into a pole of appropriate length so it hangs downward. It is important that this be clear plastic for two reasons: first, the snake may be alarmed by the solid appearance of an opaque object and less so by the more-or-less invisible appearance of the clear shield; second, you need to be able to see a snake at all times to make sure that it continues to rest calmly. The last thing you want is to give the snake an opportunity to suddenly come at you around the shield when you can't see it. Even though it means that the snake can see you too, you must always have it in view when entering its cage. This is even more true if a cage houses several specimens. It is best, therefore, that cage maintenance be a two-person job, with one person to hold the shield and, if necessary, restrain a snake with a snake hook or tongs while the other person performs the cage maintenance.

Some keepers prefer to move their snakes to a holding container. I am concerned that this may place undue stress on the snakes, but it may be safer for the keeper. However, you have to balance the risk of entering the occupied cage versus the risk involved with disturbing and moving the snakes.

Above the screened top of the cage should be an incandescent lamp of about 60 to 100 watts. Experiment with the wattage and placement of the lamp until you are able to achieve an ambient daytime temperature of about 85 to 88F (29 to 31C) at the basking spot near the top of the cage. This should be about 10 degrees F (5.5 degrees C) warmer than the lowest corner at the opposite end of the cage. This creates a nice thermal gradient and lets the snakes choose their preferred temperature. Twelve to 14 hours of light per day is good for most of the year, except for when breeding is being attempted. This helps simulate the long days of the tropics. Even if your snakes were captive-bred, their rhythms are hard-wired, and the more you can simulate natural conditions, the better.

FOOD AND WATER

Juvenile and adult Eyelash Vipers tend to be good feeders. If you obtain a specimen at least half-grown, it should be well acclimated to accepting "fuzzy" mice. This refers to mice that still have their eyes closed but are not hairless. It is not necessary to offer them alive. A frozen mouse should be thawed in warm water until limp, without ice crystals still present internally. Never microwave them—they explode, and believe me, it's no fun to

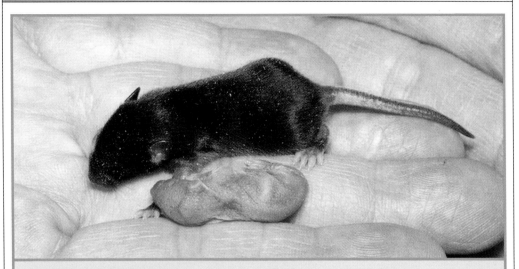

Young laboratory mice, both pinkies (without hair) and fuzzies (with hair but not yet out of the nest) are the standard food for Eyelash Vipers and other small vipers. Remember that the vipers are nocturnal and feed accordingly. Photo: M. Walls

clean up. Carefully place the warm pinkie on a branch near a perched snake by using long forceps or hemostats. If this is done just before lights-out, the snake will probably take it almost immediately. The snake may even strike as you are placing the mouse, so be cautious. Remember that these snakes are primarily nocturnal, becoming more active and doing most of their hunting at night. Some keepers with insufficient experience find that their snakes are reluctant to feed, even if teased with a warm pinkie. Most often this is because the keeper is trying to feed in the middle of the day, when all a snake wants to do is sleep. It is true that some reluctant snakes may need to be teased with food by tapping the food item gently on the snout to elicit a strike, but this is not common. Again, be very careful to use long implements and do not underestimate the strike radius of the snake. If you wish, you can experiment with placing food on the substrate. Some Eyelash Vipers may take food from the ground, but this is less reliable than placing the food closer to the snake.

Eyelash Vipers and other arboreal pitvipers may not drink reliably from a water bowl, although they may if the bowl is raised among the branches rather than resting on the substrate. In the wild they are adapted to drinking dew that condenses on plant leaves and even on their own bodies. Use a water bowl, and replace the water and sanitize the bowl on a daily basis. Even if your snakes drink from the bowl, however, they must be misted on a daily basis to maintain the proper humidity in the terrarium. Although you can gently spray a snake from above with an atomizer bottle, an interesting method that I have seen is to use an ultrasonic vaporizer. There are

Small skinks of many types are easy to find and will be taken by young Eyelash and other pitvipers. Photo: R. D. Babb

units sold for use as home humidifiers, but they are bulky and adapting them for use is a bit of a hassle. Fortunately, there are now smaller units designed specifically for herp use, and these simply drop into a good-sized water bowl. Place the bowl on the top screen of the cage and turn on the humidifier; a fine fog will start to roll out of the bowl and into the cage. (It looks a lot like dry ice special-effects fog in a horror movie and actually gives the cage a more natural "jungle" look.) Another trick sometimes used by keepers is to use an elevated bowl as described above, but with an aquarium airstone to agitate the surface and splash nearby plants from which the snakes may drink.

BREEDING

Many breeders consider the Eyelash Viper to be the easiest venomous snake to breed. Indeed, many simply keep a pair or two in the same cage and just "harvest" the litters that are born periodically. Like most (but not all!) pitvipers, the Eyelash Viper is a livebearer, with females producing from six to eight young (and rarely up to 18), in proportion to their size. Unless the cage is too small, Eyelash Vipers rarely have serious intraspecific conflicts.

Some breeders, however, consider the simple approach above to be an unreliable means of obtaining offspring and prefer to use a more systematic approach. First, the snakes are definitively sexed. Hopefully, this was done by the breeder of your original stock; if not, the snakes should be "probed" by experienced handlers—one handler restrains the head and one handler does the probing. A lubricated stainless-steel sexing probe is inserted beneath a snake's anal plate and angled backward; if the snake is a female the probe will quickly meet resistance, whereas if it is a male the probe will penetrate much further, into an inverted hemipenis. (Like all snakes and lizards, male Eyelash Vipers have a bifurcated penis that is turned inside-out and retracted behind the anal plate when the snake is not in coitus.) Sexing snakes is a tricky business, and it is easy to injure a snake if you don't know what you're doing. Add to that the danger of doing this with a venomous snake, and I will reiterate that only the very experienced should attempt it.

Once the snakes are sexed and have been kept separately and fed liberally for several months, they are prepared for breeding in a manner familiar to even the most casual snake breeder: manipulation of temperature and photoperiod (day length). However, in this case one more variable needs to be controlled: the humidity, which should be reduced from the normal 90% or more to 40% to 50%. The photoperiod in a cage containing the breeder animals is reduced to ten hours from the normal 12 to 14 hours. The temperature is also reduced, to a daytime high of only 72 to 74F (22 to 23C). The snakes may or may not feed, but they should be offered small meals every couple of weeks. Males in particular will probably go off their feed. These conditions are maintained for three months, and then the "summertime" environmental norms are re-established. Both cool-down and warm-up must be gradual; breeders recommend anywhere from several weeks to two months of incremental change.

After warm-up, the snakes' activity levels and appetites will increase. Feed them as much as they will eat, and offer the females vitamin and mineral supplementation at this time. The tendency to offer captive reptiles liberal supplementation is not as prevalent as it was several years ago, as the belief now is that keepers often over-supplemented. However, gravid female reptiles do need extra vitamins and minerals to produce strong offspring. It is also a good idea to offer calcium supplements to all snakes, young or adult, if they are being fed with pinkie or fuzzy mice, which have immature skeletons and therefore are calcium-deficient. The ratio of calcium to phosphorus in a reptilian diet should be at least 2:1, as a greater concentration of phosphorus will interfere with calcium absorption. This does not mean that the vitamin and mineral supplement you use should have this ratio. What many herp keepers failed to realize in the past was that phosphorus was already present in adequate quantities in most herp foods, including rodents, and adding more with the supplement was a bad idea. The premium supplements now on the market are phosphorus-free.

When cage conditions are fully back to the summer norms and the animals are fattened up (don't take this too literally), males are placed in the females' cages. Breeders have varying opinions on the optimum ratio of males to females. A few use one male to two or more females; many use pairs; and some prefer two males per female due to a female's relatively larger size.

You may be lucky and see copulation almost immediately,

Feeding young Eyelash Vipers sometimes can be a chore. A few keepers breed African Pygmy Mice, *Mus minutoides*, specifically to get their tiny pinkies for young vipers. Photo: M. Walls

but it is more likely that you will not witness it, as the snakes often mate at night. Don't assume that mating has not occurred just because you have not witnessed it. Rather, assume that it has occurred and prepare accordingly. About a month after the sexes were placed together, you will probably notice that the females are getting gravid. This is marked by an increase in the girth of the lower abdomen that expands anteriorly with time. Although not absolutely necessary, many breeders remove the male at this point.

Depending primarily on temperature and food supply, gestation may last three to five months, but under captive conditions it is often nearer to the low end of this range. Females may stop feeding when they are very close to delivery, perhaps because their abdomens cannot accommodate the mass of both babies and food. Reducing the size of prey offered (to small pinkie mice) may keep females feeding throughout their gestation and may reduce the time needed for a female to return to normal body weight after delivery. In the wild, Eyelash Vipers breed annually, but in captivity females have been shown to be capable of reproductive cycling in as little as seven months. Whether they *should* be bred that frequently is an open question. You will certainly get more offspring and maximize your profits (if you're being that avaricious), but some breeders are convinced that females of many reptile species that are bred frequently "burn out" and die prematurely. In other words, it may be a case of penny-wise, pound-foolish.

THE YOUNG

Neonate Eyelash Vipers are 6 to 8 inches (15 to 20 cm) at birth and weigh about 2 to 3.5 grams (roughly a tenth of an ounce). Although the neonates inject venom in proportion to their size, they are "fully functional" from birth, so don't underestimate the little tikes. Try to house them individually, as cannibalism is rare but not unknown; additionally, less dominant individuals may not get enough food if kept with siblings that feed more aggressively.

When the young are born they may not hang around in the "treetops." Juvenile *Bothriechis* of all species have been observed to spend more time on the ground than their parents. This tendency is a little less marked with Eyelash Vipers, but be aware of the possibility so that you don't get a surprise when you go to change the cage litter.

Neonates probably will not feed until their first molt, about ten days to two weeks after birth. They may be too small to take

In nature, young Eyelash Vipers feed heavily on small frogs and lizards. In captivity, some may still demand frogs such as Greenhouse Frogs, *Eleutherodactylus planirostris*, a species introduced into Florida and the Gulf Coast from tropical America. Photo: Marian Bacon

Young Eyelash Vipers and many other frog-eating snakes can be converted to pinkie mice by scenting the mice, rubbing them with the skin secretions of a fresh or frozen frog. For practical keeping, vipers must learn to accept rodents as their main food. Photo: M. Walls

pinkies of standard mice, so some keepers raise dwarf mice (a different species from the usual pet/lab mouse) to provide a source of tiny pinkies. Alternatively, some keepers feed portions of the larger pinkies rather than whole animals. However, getting the babies to accept rodents at all is sometimes troublesome. In the wild the babies feed mostly on small frogs, so they may not be keen to take warm-blooded prey from the get-go. In such cases, offer very small frogs, such as Spring Peepers, cricket frogs, or Greenhouse Frogs, or newly hatched anoles or house geckos. Offering live frogs carries the risk of transferring endoparasites, so try thawed frozen frogs first. This reduces but does not eliminate the parasitic risk. Reserve live herp prey as a last resort. An even better option is to try rubbing a small part of a pinkie, such as a tail, on a frog or lizard to pick up the scent and wean the young vipers onto rodents in this fashion. After several successful feedings this way, it often becomes unnecessary to continue scenting the pinkies.

Although no venomous snake is suitable for a beginner, the Eyelash Viper is probably the closest thing we have to a beginner's venomous snake. It is easy to obtain healthy, captive-bred babies that will grow and live for up to 20 years with proper care. So, in addition to pondering carefully whether you are ready for the challenge of a venomous snake, are you ready for the commitment with an animal that may well live longer than your dog or cat?

OTHER ARBOREAL AMERICAN PITVIPERS

Most of the *Bothriechis* that follow are quite different from the Eyelash Viper. Whereas *B. schlegeli* is most frequently found in lowland areas, the remaining species (except for the one split from *B. schlegeli*) are montane (mountain-dwelling), hailing from the cloud forests of Central America. They are generally considered more difficult to keep than Eyelash Vipers, largely because of the temperature extremes characteristic of cloud forests (hot by day, cool at night), and most of the following species are not often offered for sale to private keepers. Mexico and most other Central American nations do not export their wildlife (at least not legally), so it is unlikely that wild-caught specimens will be available frequently, if at all. Captive-breeding of these species seems to be rare outside of zoos; although there are exceptions, most zoos do not channel their excess offspring (especially venomous species) into the herp trade.

Many of the uncommonly available arboreal *Bothriechis* species come from high, often very cool, montane cloud forests of Central America. Some species are seldom collected and virtually unavailable to hobbyists. Photo: P. Freed

Above: A one-week-old Yellow-blotched Palm-Pitviper, *Bothriechis aurifer*, displays a very strong pattern. Photo: P. Freed *Below:* Adult *Bothriechis aurifer* may have the black pattern greatly reduced and be primarily green snakes with a strong black head pattern. Photo: P. Freed

Bothriechis is difficult to define without going into technicalities such as the ornamentation of the hemipenes and numbers of scales, but all are slender snakes with long, prehensile tails adapting them for an arboreal lifestyle. The canthus rostralis, the ridge from the eye to the nostril, is strongly developed, and the subcaudal scales (the scales under the tail) are not divided. No species generally is more than 32 inches (80 cm) in total length. Except for *Bothriechis schlegeli*, which extends into northwestern South America, all the other species are found between extreme southern Mexico and western Panama.

YELLOW-BLOTCHED PALM-PITVIPER
Bothriechis aurifer

B. aurifer is an attractively marked species, green with broad black stripes on the head and sometimes light spots on the dorsum (back). It is one of two montane species (the other being *B. rowleyi*) with large, shield-like scales on the top of the head. It is found in scattered montane cloud forests of central Guatemala and extreme southern Mexico. Rare specimens over 40 inches (1 meter) long have been recorded.

A female Yellow-blotched Palm-Pitviper giving birth in captivity. Notice the pattern variation in the three young. Photo: P. Freed

GUATEMALAN PALM-PITVIPER
Bothriechis bicolor

B. bicolor sometimes is not all that bicolored, but, like most of the other montane palm-pitvipers, is often a shade of green with few other markings. The head scales are very small, almost granular, and strongly keeled (each has a ridge running down its length). In this species the iris is distinctly green with black flecks. The species is found from Chiapas, Mexico, to southwestern Guatemala, plus disjunct populations in Honduras and possibly El Salvador. It prefers cloud forests and is found at elevations of up to 6600 feet (2000 meters). It also frequents overgrown coffee plantations.

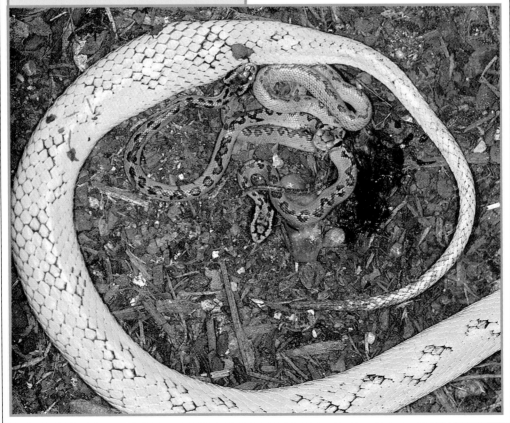

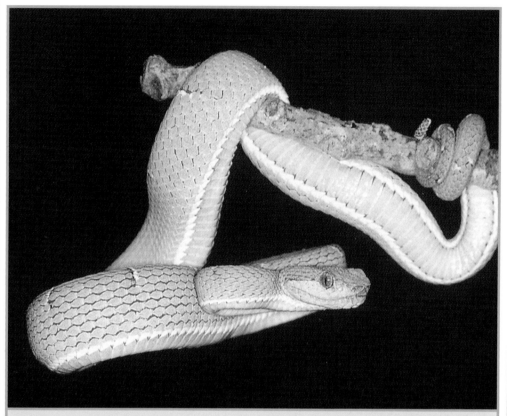

Though the body color varies from bright green to pale blue-green, the presence of narrow pale stripes on either side of the belly and the general absence of a dark head pattern make *Bothriechis lateralis*, the Side-striped Palm-Pitviper, relatively easy to recognize. Photo: P. Freed

SIDE-STRIPED PALM-PITVIPER
Bothriechis lateralis

B. *lateralis*, a species that sometimes enters the terrarium hobby, is found in the cloud forests of south-central Costa Rica south into Panama. The Side-striped Palm-Pitviper is usually green to green-blue dorsally, with an unmarked head or perhaps a faint bluish postorbital stripe. There usually is a narrow pale stripe separating the belly color from the color of the sides. This is another species that may rarely exceed 40 inches (1 meter) in length.

MARCH'S PALM-PITVIPER
Bothriechis marchi

This species is my favorite of the montane species. At first glance it appears green or blue, but on closer inspection many specimens prove to be mottled with green and sky-blue. There are many smooth, not keeled, scales on top of the snout. The iris is yellowish in adults, bronzy in young. Its range is a small area of the highlands of Honduras and perhaps adjacent Guatemala and Nicaragua on the Atlantic side. It sometimes is found at lower elevations than most other species of the genus.

Above: Most specimens of *Bothriechis marchi*, March's Palm-Pitviper, are mottled or speckled with blue and green. This may be the most colorful palm-pitviper, if you like blues. Photo: R. Hunziker *Below:* An intricate green and black pattern usually distinguishes the rare Black-speckled Palm-Pitviper, *Bothriechis nigroviridis*. This species does not seem to be closely related to the other members of its genus. Photo: P. Freed

Rowley's Palm-Pitviper, *Bothriechis rowleyi*, is restricted to extreme southern Mexico in the states of Oaxaca and perhaps Chiapas. Notice the smooth scales on the snout. Photo: P. Freed

BLACK-SPECKLED PALM-PITVIPER
Bothriechis nigroviridis

B. *nigroviridis* is sort of the odd man out among the montane palm-pitvipers. Its range overlaps that of *B. lateralis*, but it is unlikely that the species compete much in the wild. It is somewhat more restricted in distribution (central Costa Rica and western Panama) than *B. lateralis* and more rarely collected. It doesn't seem to be closely related to the other montane *Bothriechis*, which fall into two groups of apparently closely related species: *rowleyi-aurifer* and *bicolor-lateralis-marchi*. B. *nigroviridis* is relatively slender and green, but heavily peppered with black. Its bite has caused human deaths.

ROWLEY'S PALM-PITVIPER
Bothriechis rowleyi

This species is found in Oaxaca and perhaps Chiapas, Mexico. It is quite variable but usually is bright green; it tends more toward blue blotches than does its apparent closest relative, *B. aurifer*. To the best of my knowledge it has not been kept by herpetoculturists on a regular basis.

MACHOTE, TAYLOR'S PALM-PITVIPER
Bothriechis superciliaris

In 1998, Solórzano et al., redescribed the Eyelash Viper subspecies *B. schlegeli superciliaris*, originally described by Taylor in 1954, and elevated it to specific rank on the basis of color pattern, counts, and biochemical differences. This population from southwestern Costa Rica does indeed seem recognizably distinct. Specimens pictured in the redescription have a uniform ground color with well-marked, regularly spaced dorsal and/or lateral blotches. Actually, they're rather pretty. Only time will tell if the herpetological community at large accepts *B. superciliaris* as a distinct species, but who knows? It could start showing up on price lists as the "other" Eyelash Viper.

BOTHRIOPSIS

Bothriopsis is another of the genera split off from *Bothrops*. It contains at least eight species: *albocarinata, alticola, bilineata, medusa, oligolepis, peruviana, punctata,* and *taeniata.* These are found over much of northern and central South America and barely enter Panama. They are generally similar in size, appearance, habits, and care to *Bothriechis* and are usually called "forest-pitvipers" to distinguish them from their cousins. Admittedly, the names are pretty arbitrary; it's certainly possible to find palm-pitvipers in the forest and forest-pitvipers among the palms. Unlike *Bothriechis*, which has the subcaudal scales single, in this genus at least some of the subcaudals are divided in most specimens. Here we will discuss only one representative *Bothriopsis* that appears in the terrarium occasionally.

TWO-STRIPED FOREST-PITVIPER
Bothriopsis bilineata

This is the only species of the genus that currently is regularly

Species of the South American arboreal vipers placed in *Bothriopsis* seldom reach the terrarium, but a few *Bothriopsis taeniata* are occasionally seen. The relatively dull camouflage coloration makes this snake hard to see. Photo: R. D. Bartlett

Above: **This stunningly colored Two-striped Forest-Pitviper,** *Bothriopsis bilineata,* **represents the nominate subspecies,** *B. b. bilineata,* **from coastal forests of Venezuela, the Guianas, and Brazil.** Photo: R. D. Bartlett *Below:* **The heavily black-speckled back marks this as** *Bothriopsis bilineata smaragdina,* **the subspecies found in much of the Amazon basin and adjacent highlands of South America.** Photo: P. Freed

kept and bred by herpetoculturists. (This may change, however; there certainly are people working with other species.) The Two-Lined Forest-Pitviper is found over most of northern South America, particularly throughout the Amazon basin, and also along the coast of southeastern Brazil. They are a light green to powder-blue in color, often with lime green or yellow on the labials and on the belly. The flank color is separated from the ventral color by a thin white stripe on each side (thus *bilineata*, meaning "two-striped"). Some specimens have evenly spaced greenish yellow spots on the dorsum or flanks. Adult size, captive care, and breeding closely parallel those of the Eyelash Viper. The young are very small and have relatively narrow heads;

they may escape if the cage screening does not have a small mesh size.

For details on how to distinguish the many species of *Bothriechis* and *Bothriopsis*, get a copy of *The Venomous Reptiles of Latin America* by J. A. Campbell and W. W. Lamar (1989, Cornell University Press). This book covers all the venomous snakes from Mexico to South America, illustrating most in color and with excellent range maps.

THE TEMPLE VIPER,
Tropidolaemus wagleri

THE PITVIPER OF GOOD FORTUNE

The Temple of the Azure Cloud is a world-famous destination for travelers visiting Penang, Malaysia. More commonly and appropriately known as the Snake Temple, it is home to large groups of Temple Vipers, *Tropidolaemus wagleri*. The snakes are considered to bring good fortune, perhaps one of the few places outside India where a venomous snake is revered rather than reviled. It is claimed that the snakes come to the temple naturally, but the temple's population is also supplemented by collectors from more rural areas. The Taoist priests of the Snake Temple revere and care for the snakes, feeding them fish. Worshipers and visitors also leave chicken eggs that the snakes consume. The snakes seem quite placid, and the priests may even free-handle them. Some Western observers have speculated that the heavy use of incense in the

A colorful male Malaysian phase Temple Viper, *Tropidolaemus wagleri*. The common name comes from its association with the Snake Temple of Penang, Malaysia. Photo: R. D. Bartlett

This female (Sulawesi phase) Temple Viper shows the major attributes of the genus *Tropidolaemus*: the strong ridge from eye to snout, keeled scales on the head, and nasal scales not fused to the first supralabial scale. Photo: R. D. Bartlett

temple may contribute to calming the snakes. Visitors can even have their pictures taken while holding "defanged" snakes, which have been marked with paint to distinguish them from the other snakes in the temple. (You can try it if you like. Not me!)

Perhaps the mystical aura associated with this snake is part of its appeal with herpetoculturists. It also doesn't hurt that the species is gorgeous, of decent size, and relatively easy to keep. It is a close second to the Eyelash Viper in terms of popularity, and the often higher price tag of a well-marked Temple Viper is perhaps the only reason it doesn't own the top spot.

A UNIQUE SPECIES

Tropidolaemus is a small genus split off from the bamboo vipers, genus *Trimeresurus*, which we will consider a little later. For a long time *T. wagleri* was the only species in the genus, but in 1998 David and Vogel redescribed *Trimeresurus huttoni* from southern India (originally described by Smith in 1949) and then placed it in *Tropidolaemus*.

The Temple Viper (also called Wagler's Viper or Wagler's Temple Viper) hails from Malaysia, Indonesia, and the Philippines. *Tropidolaemus* is usually distinguished from *Trimeresurus* in the broad sense by having the canthus rostralis (ridge from eye to tip of snout) strongly defined, the top of the head covered with strongly keeled scales (smooth in *Trimeresurus*), and the nasal scute (around the nostril) not fused to the first supralabial or upper lip scale; the subcaudal scales are paired.

It is a strikingly colored but variable snake. Some specimens are solid green, some are green with thin white bands, and some are blackish with cream to yellow crossbands and a white or yellow center in the middle of nearly every dark scale. Juveniles have a fascinating and unusual color pattern: they are emerald-green with evenly spaced pairs of spots that are half red, half white, as well as a similarly bicolored facial stripe. Although intermediates are often seen, there are four generally accepted races of *T. wagleri*: Kalimantan, Malaysian, Philippine, and Sulawesi. The Kalimantan (Borneo) phase seems to be the most favored because it has a strong tendency toward bluish coloration and very little if any black. The Malaysian phase is multicolored; most of the specimens at the Snake Temple are of this race. The Philippine race is interesting because it is a dwarf, half the size of the other races; it also retains a juvenile color pattern into adulthood. The Sulawesi (Celebes) phase is green with sparse, narrow white and/or blue barring.

A Kalimantan (Borneo) phase female Temple Viper. This phase often is strongly blue-tinted, with very little black. Photo: R. D. Bartlett

Above: A Malaysian (Sumatran) phase female Temple Viper. In this common phase there is much black, yellow, green, and sometimes red in the pattern. Photo: R. D. Bartlett
Below: Adults of the Philippine phase are generally multicolored like the Malaysian phase but tend to be much smaller, with a juvenile-like pattern. Photo: Z. Takacs

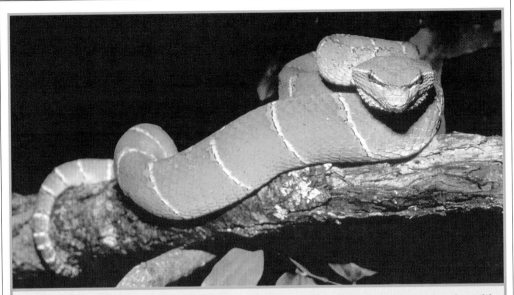

A Sulawesi (Celebes) phase female Temple Viper showing the overall green color with narrow pale barring typical of the form. It would not be surprising if the major phases of Temple Viper were eventually distinguished as full species. Photo: R. D. Bartlett

As with the other arboreal vipers, females are larger than males, but the difference is far more pronounced in this species. Males are much shorter, of course, but also remain very slender, and a fully grown female may weigh several times more than a male. Although it can sometimes be difficult to tell juveniles and males apart, there is no doubt with mature females. On average, adult males seldom exceed 22 inches (55 cm) in length, while adult females are 32 to 38 inches (80 to 95 cm) long.

Captives seem lazier than Eyelash Vipers and sometimes rest on the same perch without apparent motion for days on end. This can be deceiving, however, as the snakes can strike with alarming speed, and often do so if anything enters their strike radius. They are most likely to be active at night or under low-light conditions.

Unlike Eyelash Vipers, which can frequently be kept in groups with little or no trouble, Temple Vipers are often very aggressive toward others of their kind unless the enclosure is large. In addition, well-established animals get a bit set in their ways and may even kill a newly introduced specimen. Temple Vipers can be kept together, but it is best to use a very large enclosure (30 to 40 gallons, 114 to 152 L, of volume for each adult female, and about 20 gallons, 76 L, of volume for each male) and to introduce all of the snakes at one time, so that no individual has squatter's rights. If you must introduce a new specimen, remove the established snake and then place the new one in the cage for several days by itself. By the time you reintroduce the original snake, the new one should have enough of a foothold on territory, so to speak. It is also helpful if the cage has

Temple Vipers tend to be territorial, so some care is needed when trying to keep two specimens together. The very large head of the species compared to the slender body is obvious here. Photo: R. D. Bartlett

Because of their moderate size and general inactivity during the day, Temple Vipers are not difficult to house or care for. Remember, however, that at night they may become very aggressive and dangerous animals. Photo: R. D. Bartlett

many plants to create visual barriers, as the snakes will not usually perch within sight of each other unless it is unavoidable. This strong territoriality is probably also the reason that many keepers report that these vipers are quick to strike when their space is invaded, but once removed from the cage they calm down and are much easier to manipulate.

Keep in mind that all arboreal vipers may seem downright schizophrenic with regard to their changes in mood. A snake that is placid by day may be irritable and quick(er) to strike at night. As we noted when discussing Eyelash Vipers, when you consider the nocturnal preferences of arboreal vipers this should be no surprise, as they hunt by night and will therefore be more alert and aggressive, not to mention that

they probably don't like having you turn on the lights when they are active.

CARE AND BREEDING

The captive care of *T. wagleri* is essentially similar to that of the Eyelash Viper. However, some keepers have reported that the snakes become jittery if they are hydrated via a fine mist, such as with the ultrasonic vaporizers we discussed for *Bothriechis*. Spritzing them with a spray bottle often seems less annoying; however, the wise keeper will not squirt a snake directly in the face. It has been suggested that mating may be induced by creating a simulation of the wet season following a drier season, misting the terrarium heavily for several days. The snakes have also been noted to breed in response to sudden

Selective breeding has resulted in the presence of some truly stunning Temple Vipers in the hobby. This blue morph female is derived from the Kalimantan phase. Photo: P. Freed

changes in barometric pressure, as when fronts move in during severe thunderstorms.

Breeding is also similar to the strategies reported for *B. schlegeli*, but the greater territoriality of *T. wagleri* must be considered and plans made to separate potential mates if they prove incompatible. Due to the much greater size of the female, this species should always be bred via a "reverse trio" arrangement: two males per female. Litter size varies from fewer than a dozen to nearly two dozen young.

Temple Vipers have a tendency to develop respiratory infections, so watch the humidity level and avoid drafts. They also have a tendency toward constipation but can be encouraged to defecate by soaking for several hours in warm water. Make sure the water is no more than an inch (2.5 cm) or so deep and provide a rock or ramp that will allow the snake to rest its head out of the water without effort. Obesity also is a problem with this very lethargic species, so restrict feeding to one mouse a week if you think your specimens are gaining too much weight.

The bite from the Temple Viper is painful though it seems to have not caused human deaths. That this is a virtually harmless snake is as much a myth as that the bite of the Eyelash Viper is no worse than a bee sting. The bite of small vipers, regardless of size and species, can never be treated lightly. The best bet is to always be cautious when cleaning the cage, feeding, or moving snakes and just avoid being bitten.

For an excellent article on the joys and foibles of Temple Vipers, see R. D. Bartlett, 1997, *Reptile Hobbyist*, 3(3), November.

THE BAMBOO VIPERS

ASIAN *TRIMERESURUS*

Although sometimes they have also been called "palm vipers" along with their Neotropical cousins, here we will use the more recent convention of referring to the genus *Trimeresurus* primarily as "bamboo vipers." Be aware that you may see either name in other literature, as well as other variations. Despite a few attempts at international standardization of the common names of herps, there is no universally accepted source, so we do the best we can.

Trimeresurus are confusing, to say the least. There are at least 35 species, depending on how you split them, and they include both heavy-bodied, ground-dwelling snakes and a plethora of medium-sized arboreal species that mostly seem to be some shade of green. Geographic origin is important when trying to identify "trims," as many keepers call them. Unfortunately, some that are bred and sold are misidentified, and some of the photos in books are misidentified as well (maybe even this one; although we try hard for accurate identification, these are hard snakes indeed).

The ground-dwelling *Trimeresurus* are a curious group. Most of these go by the native name of *habu*. They are often dull-colored—brown or gray with

Many species of *Trimeresurus* are relatively dull, heavy-set terrestrial species, but there are colorful forms throughout the genus. *Trimeresurus flavomaculatus* from the Philippines, for instance, includes some of the most colorful pitvipers known. Photo: P. Freed

darker crossbars or diamonds—
and tend to be irritable, so they
are not popular with
herpetoculturists. The really odd
thing about them is that they are
egglayers and guard their eggs.
Because they are not livebearers
like almost all the rest of the
members of the genus (indeed,
almost all the rest of the
pitvipers), the species *chaseni,
flavoviridis, monticola,
okinavensis, tonkinensis*, and
zayuensis are often referred to the
genus *Ovophis* (literally, "egg
snake"). However, egglaying
versus livebearing as a mode of
reproduction does not necessarily
justify a separate genus. There
are even reptiles in which the
lowland populations are egglaying
and the highland populations
livebearing—in the same species!

Some research indicates that the
arboreal and terrestrial trims are
not sufficiently distinct to be
placed in separate genera, despite
their reproductive differences. My
advice is to let the professional
herpetologists argue over this one.
The tree-dwelling trims are "where
it's at" in herpetoculture, anyway.
However, I should mention that
there may be at least one egglayer
among the tree-dwellers too, *T.
hageni.*

The arboreal trims are greatly
feared in many areas where they
occur. Many are called "100-pace
snakes" by the locals because
supposedly a person who is bitten
will drop dead after taking less
than 100 steps. Even worse,
according to local lore in Vietnam,
is *T. albolabris*, which is known as
the "two-step death." In reality,

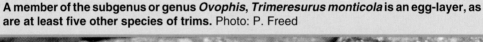

A member of the subgenus or genus *Ovophis, Trimeresurus monticola* is an egg-layer, as are at least five other species of trims. Photo: P. Freed

A typical green bamboo viper, *Trimeresurus albolabris* perhaps more often is available as wild-collected rather than captive-bred specimens. Photo: R. D. Bartlett

although some *Trimeresurus* have caused human fatalities, especially in rural areas of Southeast Asia, and none should be taken lightly, with proper medical attention almost all bites are survivable.

Many trims, particularly juveniles, have red to maroon tails. Interestingly, some observations indicate that they may use this for caudal luring in a fashion similar to that seen in young moccasins and cantils (the American members of the genus *Agkistrodon*). Waving the colorful, slender tail tip may attract small prey such as the treefrogs that form a large part of the diet of young trims in the wild. Young *Bothriechis* and *Bothriopsis* have also been known to engage in luring behavior.

The care of trims is virtually identical to that of the American arboreal pitvipers. We will not attempt to cover all of the species here; many are absent from herpetoculture and some are not even scientifically well known. Let's take a look at several of the more common species that are bred and traded in varying quantities.

WHITE-LIPPED BAMBOO VIPER
Trimeresurus albolabris

The most available of the trims in herpetoculture is *T. albolabris*, a species found from India and Nepal to southern China and Indonesia. It is often available

Above: Identifying the green bamboo vipers is a challenge even to herpetologists, and it is possible that many of the snakes in the terrarium hobby are misidentified to some extent. This green beauty is *Trimeresurus erythrurus*, the Red-tailed Bamboo Viper. Photo: W. Wüster *Below:* Checking details of head scalation often is important in identifying bamboo vipers. In this *Trimeresurus erythrurus* the scales on the snout are very small and the supralabials (scales of the upper lip) are fused into just a few large scales. Photo: W. Wüster

inexpensively, but some specimens offered for sale are wild-caught. It is better to pay more for a captive-bred snake than to go to the effort of acclimating, rehydrating, and deparasitizing a wild-caught snake, which will probably end up costing more in the long run. In much of the literature and in more than a few published photos, this species has been confused with *T. stejnegeri* and *T. popeiorum*. However, they can be distinguished on the basis of the fusion of the nasal and first (upper) labial scale in *T. albolabris*; the other two species lack this feature (however, the very similar *T. erythrurus* also displays this scale fusion, so be careful). This species is hardy and grows large, with females reaching up to 40 inches (1 meter). Although it is not quite a "two-step death," it is a formidable snake and not to be underestimated.

RED-TAILED BAMBOO VIPER
Trimeresurus erythrurus

This species is no more red-tailed than the other all-green trims, but it has garnered the common name all the same. Red-Tailed Bamboo Vipers come in varying shades of green, but most are a bit on the dark side. It shares with several other species the male characteristic of the white or red ventrolateral stripes, but in this species the red stripe is very thin and easy to overlook. Females lack the red stripe, and a minority of males may lack it also. This is a large trim, with females reaching up to 48 inches (122 cm). This species is considered to have more deadly potential than some other

Their large fangs and often aggressive temperaments make the bamboo vipers more dangerous than their small size might indicate. Photo: *Trimeresurus erythrurus*, R. D. Bartlett

trims, in part because of its size. (However, I stress again that for safety's sake all arboreal vipers should be considered potentially deadly.) As might be expected from its size, it is also relatively more prolific than some of its congeners, with broods of up to 17 young recorded. Red-tails are basically Indian but occur east to Burma.

INDIAN BAMBOO VIPER
Trimeresurus gramineus

A potentially useful feature in identifying this species is that it tends to have both keeled and smooth scales (most other trims have only keeled scales). It is found from south-central India to Malaysia, with subspecies on Sumatra and Kalimantan (Borneo), and prefers lowland areas near running water. Specimens may be bronze, pale green, or a combination of colors; the tail is often dark red. Litters average six to eight 8-inch young.

HAGEN'S BAMBOO VIPER
Trimeresurus hageni

Females of this species that ranges from Thailand to Indonesia can grow to 36 inches (91 cm), but males are much smaller, topping out at only 24 inches (61 cm). Both sexes are bright blue-green with a row of round to oval

Trimeresurus gramineus, the Indian Bamboo Viper, actually has a gigantic range extending from India to Sumatra and Borneo. Photo: S. Kochetov

dots down each flank, often not quite symmetrical relative to the midbody axis. There is a white to pinkish postorbital stripe. Both sexes usually have a white ventrolateral stripe. There may be some red tipping to the insides (ventrally) of these scales in males; however, it's not seen in all specimens and probably should not be considered a reliable indicator of sex (as it is in *T. popeiorum* and *T. stejnegeri*, for example).

Unlike most of the other arboreal trims, this is supposedly an oviparous species, laying something on the order of 17 eggs. There is currently little herpetocultural experience with this species, although some are being kept, but hopefully we will soon know more about this enigmatic species.

POPE'S BAMBOO VIPER
Trimeresurus popeiorum

India, Myanmar (Burma), Malaysia, and Indonesia are home to this species. Adults are similar in size to other arboreal trims and are usually a bright emerald-green, somewhat paler on the labials, with little or no other patterning. Females grow to about 30 inches (76 cm) and males to slightly over 24 inches (61 cm). Litters range up to 12 in number but are more often in the range of six or seven 7-inch babies. A characteristic shared by several of the all-green trims, but which is perhaps most distinct in this species, is that males have a white ventrolateral (that is, right at the scale row where the belly

Above: Hagen's Bamboo Viper, *Trimeresurus hageni*, often has more pattern elements than some other bamboo vipers, including a pale stripe behind the eye and pale spots on the body. Photo: R. D. Bartlett *Below:* There are several "all green" bamboo vipers that show little or no pattern other than a white stripe on the lower sides (plus a red one in males). This is thought to be *Trimeresurus popeiorum*, Pope's Bamboo Viper. Photo: P. Donovan

meets the flank) stripe, with a red stripe of roughly equal width below it. A thinner double stripe of this type may occur behind the eye, but with the colors reversed (red above white). Females have the white ventrolateral stripe, but no red one.

PURPLE-SPOTTED BAMBOO VIPER
Trimeresurus purpureomaculatus

This is a foul-tempered beast as trims go. However, it is also very hardy and does have its fans among keepers. It is a bit more terrestrial than most other trims but does spend a lot of time climbing too. It is nearly as heavy-bodied as the terrestrial *"Ovophis"* trims. The species ranges from Thailand to Malaysia and Sumatra, where it preferentially inhabits mangrove estuaries. It is a large species, reaching up to 44 inches (110 cm). There are two phases of the Purple-spotted Bamboo Viper. One is red-brown to burnt orange above, with an orange belly. Such snakes vaguely remind me of Red-Bellied Water Snakes (*Nerodia erythrogaster*) from the eastern U.S. The other phase has a more reticulated pattern, purplish brown overall with purple-centered scales down to the ventrolaterals, which often have cream-colored centers; the belly is dirty white. Litters range from 3 to 16; the babies are about 8 inches long. They feed aggressively on pinkie mice.

STEJNEGER'S BAMBOO VIPER
Trimeresurus stejnegeri

Also known as the Chinese Bamboo Viper, *T. stejnegeri* is

Though not very colorful and noted for a vicious temper, the stout-bodied Purple-spotted Bamboo Viper, *Trimeresurus purpureomaculatus*, is fairly common in the terrarium hobby. Photo: R. D. Bartlett

Trimeresurus purpureomaculatus generally is more common in mangrove thickets than in bamboo thickets, which may explain its darker, browner coloration. Photo: Z. Takacs

found from Nepal and northern Burma eastward over much of southern China and southeast to Vietnam and Thailand; it also is found on Taiwan. There are several described subspecies that in recent years sometimes have been considered full species (e.g., *T. yunnanensis*). *T. stejnegeri* is often confused with *T. popeiorum*, and it may take counting scale rows to distinguish them, but even then there is some overlap that may cause uncertainty. *T. popeiorum* has 23 or 21 midbody scale rows, whereas *T. stejnegeri* has 19 or 21. *T. stejnegeri* tends to be more of a bronze-green than *T. popeiorum*, but this is not reliable enough to distinguish the species. A more reliable method, though a bit tricky, is to check the

The presence of a bright red line under the white line on the lower side indicates that this almost certainly is a male. The species is *Trimeresurus stejnegeri*, Stejneger's Bamboo Viper. Photo: W. Wüster

Trimeresurus stejnegeri **is one of the more common green bamboo vipers in the terrarium. To tell it from** *T. popeiorum* **with certainty requires checking the hemipenes of an adult male, not always an easy task with a venomous snake.** Photo: R. D. Bartlett

hemipenis, which is spiny in *T. stejnegeri* and smooth in *T. popeiorum*. This is most easily done on juveniles, in which gently pressing the base of the tail below the vent can "pop" the hemipenis. This is also a good way to sex young snakes without probing. However, like probing, it is easy to harm a snake if you don't know what you're doing. In the wild, *T. stejnegeri* is found in bamboo brush along streams, where it hunts frogs. In captivity it adapts well to pinkie and fuzzy mice, although neonates may need some coaxing.

SUMATRAN BAMBOO VIPER
Trimeresurus sumatranus

Unlike most of the trims, which take birds and mammals mostly opportunistically, the Sumatran Bamboo Viper seems to prefer them. Like most of the trims, it grows to roughly 36 inches (91 cm). Most specimens are light green with a brown to reddish tail and cream to yellow labials, throat, and belly. As you would expect from the name, it is found on Sumatra and adjacent islands, but it also occurs on Kalimantan (Borneo) and on the mainland north to Thailand.

SRI LANKAN BAMBOO VIPER
Trimeresurus trigonocephalus

Coming from mountain forests and tea plantations of Sri Lanka, this is without a doubt the prettiest of the trims, but it is a rarity that commands a pretty penny when you find it offered for sale. Folks who fancy them often call them "trigs." The scales are light green to turquoise, and the interstitial skin (between the scales) is black. The dorsum is usually marked with black diamonds, and there is a black wedge that begins roughly at the

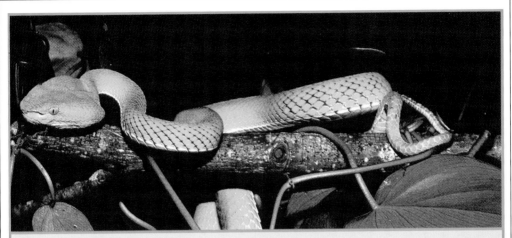

Above: A female Sumatran Bamboo Viper, *Trimeresurus sumatranus.* Photo: R. D. Bartlett, court. M. Stuhlman *Below:* The heavily marked Sri Lankan Bamboo Viper, *Trimeresurus trigonocephalus*, may bear a close resemblance to some American palm-pitvipers, *Bothriechis.* Photo: P. Freed

eye and expands broadly toward the back of the head. Females can grow to 36 inches (91 cm); males reach about 32 inches (80 cm). This species seems more willing than other trigs to drink from a water bowl, even one kept on the ground. They are aggressive feeders if fed at night, but by day they are reluctant to strike at prey. These snakes can be kept communally with little aggressive interaction, but there is one exception, and it applies to all arboreal vipers: when feeding, in addition to keeping your hands out of the strike zone, make sure that they do not attack each other, as they can become quite excited when their companions are eating. They may bite each other or, more likely, seize

Trimeresurus venustus **formerly was widely known as** *Trimeresurus kanburiensis* **and still is called the Kanburian Bamboo Viper. Purple- and green-barred specimens like this one are females.** Photo: Suzanne L. Collins

opposite ends of the same prey item, leading to a case of more-or-less accidental cannibalism. Neonates are about 8 inches long when born, and feed on treefrogs. However, captive-bred young usually feed well on small pinkie mice offered every two weeks. Adults should be fed only every three to four weeks. As with much of Sri Lanka's wildlife, this species is considered threatened in the wild. There have been no imports for years (as it should be, given their current status), and all specimens currently available to herpetoculturists are captive-bred. Breeders and zoos should be encouraged to make even more of an effort to preserve this handsome viper.

KANBURIAN BAMBOO VIPER
Trimeresurus venustus

Formerly called *T. kanburiensis*, this is an unusually colored species: females are barred with green and purple, while males have less purple but have distinct white and red ventrolateral stripes. Because the color differences are consistent (sexual dichromatism, a type of sexual dimorphism), it usually is not a problem to distinguish the sexes. The sexes also differ in size: females reach 30 inches (76 cm), males just 24 inches (61 cm). It hails from Thailand and is quite rare in collections at the present time, as Thailand does not export its wildlife any longer. This species has often been confused with *T. purpureomaculatus*, but it displays a distinctive enlargement of the first three upper labials that is lacking in the Purple-Spotted Bamboo Viper. Litters range from 2 to 16 in number, and babies are 6 to 8 inches long at birth.

LEGAL, ETHICAL, AND MEDICAL ISSUES

I have probably been harping on it to the point of overkill, but I want to say it again: owning venomous snakes is not for everybody. In fact, it's not for almost everybody. Keeping "hot" serpents carries a level of responsibility not to be taken lightly—you must be able to ensure that you, your family, your friends, and your local community will be safe from your charges. Having a venomous snake is very much like having a loaded gun in the house, except that you can't "unload" the snake. In this chapter I want to carefully examine the very real issues that are attached to the keeping of venomous snakes, because they directly impact you if you are even entertaining the notion of keeping them.

I am really neither for nor against the keeping of venomous snakes, but it takes a special person to deal with them safely. Even the experts have accidents, so you have to consider the worst-case scenarios and ponder what you will do if you are bitten.

No matter how small or how beautiful, Eyelash Vipers and their relatives are not keepable by everyone. They are dangerous snakes and seldom fit into a household situation. Photo: R. D. Babb

ETHICAL ISSUES

I will do a little bit more preaching here, so forgive me, but in my opinion there are situations in which the keeping of venomous snakes crosses the line of ethical, responsible behavior, and I will resist any attempt to convince me otherwise. A few examples follow.

*You must *never* keep venomous snakes if you live in an apartment or other rental housing or if your home is physically attached to a neighbor's home (for example, a duplex).

*You must *never* keep venomous snakes in the same dwelling with children. If you have kids, you must not have these snakes in your home. I don't care how many security precautions you take.

*You must *never* keep venomous snakes if you are a minor.

*You must *never* keep these snakes in unlocked cages. If the cage does not have a security lock (and I mean key or combination), it's not good enough.

*You must *never* attempt to free-handle your snakes (i.e., the kind of loose, unrestrained handling you might do with a Corn Snake). Although many venomous snakes become fairly docile, they can never be trusted.

*You must *never* handle venomous snakes or do cage maintenance under the influence of alcohol or other drugs that reduce reaction time. It's surprising how many cases of amateur keepers bitten by their hot snakes have had alcohol as a compounding factor.

*Confirm that it is in fact legal to keep venomous snakes in your area. Many states/provinces and cities specifically outlaw the keeping of venomous snakes, and many others at least have vague "dangerous animal" ordinances that would certainly apply. Don't think that you can ignore the local laws and that no one will ever find out, because you are in a lot of trouble if they do.

*If it is legal to keep venomous snakes, it is not necessarily legal to sell them, which may throw a monkey wrench into your breeding plans. If permits are required, make sure you have them and that they are kept up to date.

I could go on, but I think you're getting the idea.

KEEPING IT SAFE

The most important consideration in keeping hot snakes is preventing them from escaping. Anyone who has kept even nonvenomous snakes for a few years has probably had an escape or two. I know I have! There is no margin for error with hot snakes. They must be kept in *locked* cages (key or combination lock) with no cover or door loose enough to be pushed open. This means that the covers and/or doors of the cage must be an integral part of the cage, not "add-ons." An aquarium with a screen top, however tight-fitting it may be, is *not* acceptable. Any ventilation mesh must also be considered for its "escapability." Quarter-inch (6-mm) mesh will certainly prevent an adult snake from escaping, but some species produce babies small enough to squeeze through. I recommend that no mesh be smaller than one-eighth-inch (3-mm).

Consider entry into the hot room. The room must have a locking door, and there can be no space between the floor and the wall or under the door that would allow a snake to get out of the room. An airlock-type arrangement of double doors is even better, as it would prevent a snake from scooting out and escaping the second you open the door. The downside to this is that you may be confined in a small space with an angry snake. For an even greater degree of safety, consider using heavy glass doors, as seeing into the hot room before you enter is the best way to avoid a nasty surprise. Make sure that snake hooks, tongs, and other handling implements are in easy reach the moment you enter. You might even want to carry one snake hook when you enter rather than enter the room "unarmed."

Ventilation ductwork must be in the ceiling, not along the floor. It is also helpful to have the cages clustered toward the center of the room, not along the walls, and well off the floor; this prevents an escaped snake from squeezing into an inaccessible location behind or under a row of cages. Don't stack boxes or create other obstructions on the floor. Basically, you want to make absolutely sure that if a snake escapes from its cage it cannot escape from the room and that there is enough space to deal with it out in the open.

Even clothing should be considered. Always wear loose-fitting long pants of heavy fabric, such as blue jeans. As for shirts, you will have to decide whether you prefer the slight extra protection of a long-sleeved shirt or the greater mobility your arm may have in a short-sleeved shirt. Finally, wear high-topped leather boots. These precautions should help increase the odds (slightly!) that a snake will end up with a mouthful of something besides you if there is an accident.

Use a mental safety checklist when entering or leaving the "hot room" and have a written list of procedures to follow in the event of a snakebite, including vital information such as emergency phone numbers. Open the door cautiously, scanning the floor, then enter quickly and shut the door. Do a complete scan of the floor. Do a headcount of all snakes in their cages. Only when you have confirmed that all are present and accounted for are you actually ready to do cage maintenance and other chores. Replacing a water dish can be done with tongs, but any more involved cage maintenance should be done with the snake OUT of the cage and secure somewhere else. Finally, when you leave the room, do another headcount and check that all cages are locked, then close and lock the door.

With the types of safety measures I'm recommending here, it probably sounds like the Level 4 biocontainment they use for the Ebola virus! What's next? Rubber spacesuits? Actually, the analogy is real. In both cases we are talking about containing dangerous organisms—those that can kill you or others if they are permitted to escape. Having the mindset that your snake room is "the hot zone" is the first, best step toward avoiding mishaps.

Be cautious of who you let visit your snake room. Only people as experienced as you should enter. The room should not be a tourist attraction, or mishaps may occur. Speaking of mishaps, do you have a large amount of liability insurance? Don't think that any normal homeowner's insurance policy will cover your snakes and any accident you might have with them. You *must* find insurance that specifically acknowledges your hot snakes and insures you against accidents involving them, especially accidents involving other people. It will cost you a pretty penny, and it will probably take you a long time to find an insurer willing to write such a policy. Another insurance issue to consider is whether your medical insurance would cover you if you were bitten by one of your snakes. It is possible that it would not. Emergency care, antivenin injections, and a hospital stay could run into very large sums.

MEDICAL RESPONSIBILITY

Next, let's consider some medical aspects. Remember that all of the snakes we've covered in this book have the potential (though sometimes slight) to kill you, and it is nearly certain that you will be permanently injured, at the very least, if you are bitten. Even the Eyelash Viper, which is often considered one of the least venomous of the arboreal vipers, has caused at least one fatality.

The bite from any *Bothriechis*, *Bothriopsis*, or *Trimeresurus* will likely result in heavy tissue damage, a hospital stay, and the loss of use of the bitten area. Even small pitvipers are dangerous, and all have bad days when they may be unexpectedly aggressive. Photo: Z. Takacs

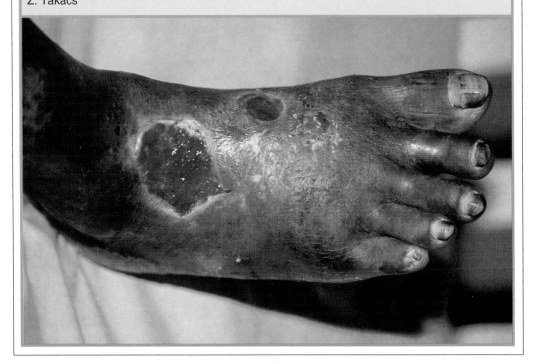

This is not a harmless snake! If you are bitten by one of your charges, it will most likely be on a finger, and the massive local tissue damage that results often necessitates amputation of the digit, even if you receive immediate medical attention and injections of antivenin. Even if the digit survives, there often is permanent damage that reduces its range of motion.

You should keep appropriate antivenin (sometimes called antivenom) for all the species with which you are working. Although zoos will have antivenin for the snakes they keep, don't assume that medical personnel will be able to obtain antivenin if you are bitten. Antivenin is expensive, must be kept refrigerated, and has a limited shelf life (generally several years). Also, antivenin is not available for every species of venomous snake. Fortunately, Wyeth-Ayerst Laboratories in Philadelphia manufactures Crotalidae Polyvalent, a combined antivenin effective against most Neotropical pitvipers, including *Bothriechis* and *Bothriopsis*. There is also a polyvalent antivenin available that covers *Trimeresurus*.

Keep in mind that antivenins are not without their drawbacks. Most are produced from purified horse serum, and some people who are injected will have a severe allergic response, perhaps even fatal anaphylactic shock. Antivenins must therefore be administered only by trained medical personnel under controlled conditions with monitoring of vital signs.

I hope I didn't lose anybody with this chapter. I probably sounded a bit harsh, but I don't want you to have any illusions about the very serious issues involved with the keeping of hot snakes. Am I being paranoid? Absolutely not! Once again, I stress that there is no margin for error with hot snakes. These snakes are not for the casual hobbyist, but I would hate to see them legislated out of existence and made inaccessible to those with a serious interest in studying their biology and captive care. However, keepers of hot snakes *must* behave responsibly.

IN CONCLUSION

Thus we end our short look at the arboreal pitvipers of the Neotropics and southern Asia. I hope that you leaned something, and I'll let you in on a secret—I learned a lot too. When writing a book, I'm forced to re-evaluate everything I know or *think* I know about the topic. I know that we have made tremendous strides in recent years in our understanding of the natural history and captive care of the arboreal pitvipers, but we still have a long way to go.

I hope that by now you have a deeper appreciation and understanding of these snakes. Maybe, just maybe, if you have enough experience and the proper respectful attitude toward these beautiful but dangerous animals, you might consider the keeping and breeding of Eyelash Vipers or Temple Vipers. I can't go so far as to encourage you do so, but a very select few of you out there just might have what it takes.

INDEX

Page numbers in **bold** indicate photos